For Ben and Maddie:
as different as mist and mud puddles.

God Made Every Person Unique!
Text © 2025 Sally Apokedak
Illustrations © 2025 Ellen Injerd
Published by Paraklesis Press
Designed by Sally Apokedak
ISBN: 978-1-947446-40-3

God Made

Every Person

Unique

Sally Apokedak ~ illustrated by Ellen Injerd

People are different as daytime
    from night—
Some noisy, while some
    rarely speak.
Some are left-handed and
    others are right ...
God made every person unique!

Some folks love mornings—
   there's no time to lose!
They get out of bed
   with a leap.
Others might snuggle
   in blankets and snooze.
They just need
   a little more sleep.

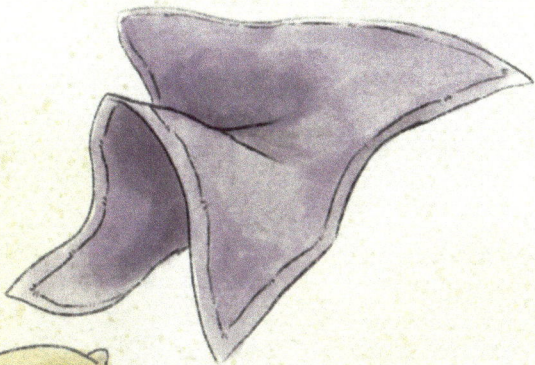

Daddy's hot pancakes
make Saturdays sweet ...

Or maybe sliced fruit fits your mood.
We have our favorites that we love to eat.
God gives us such tasty, good food!

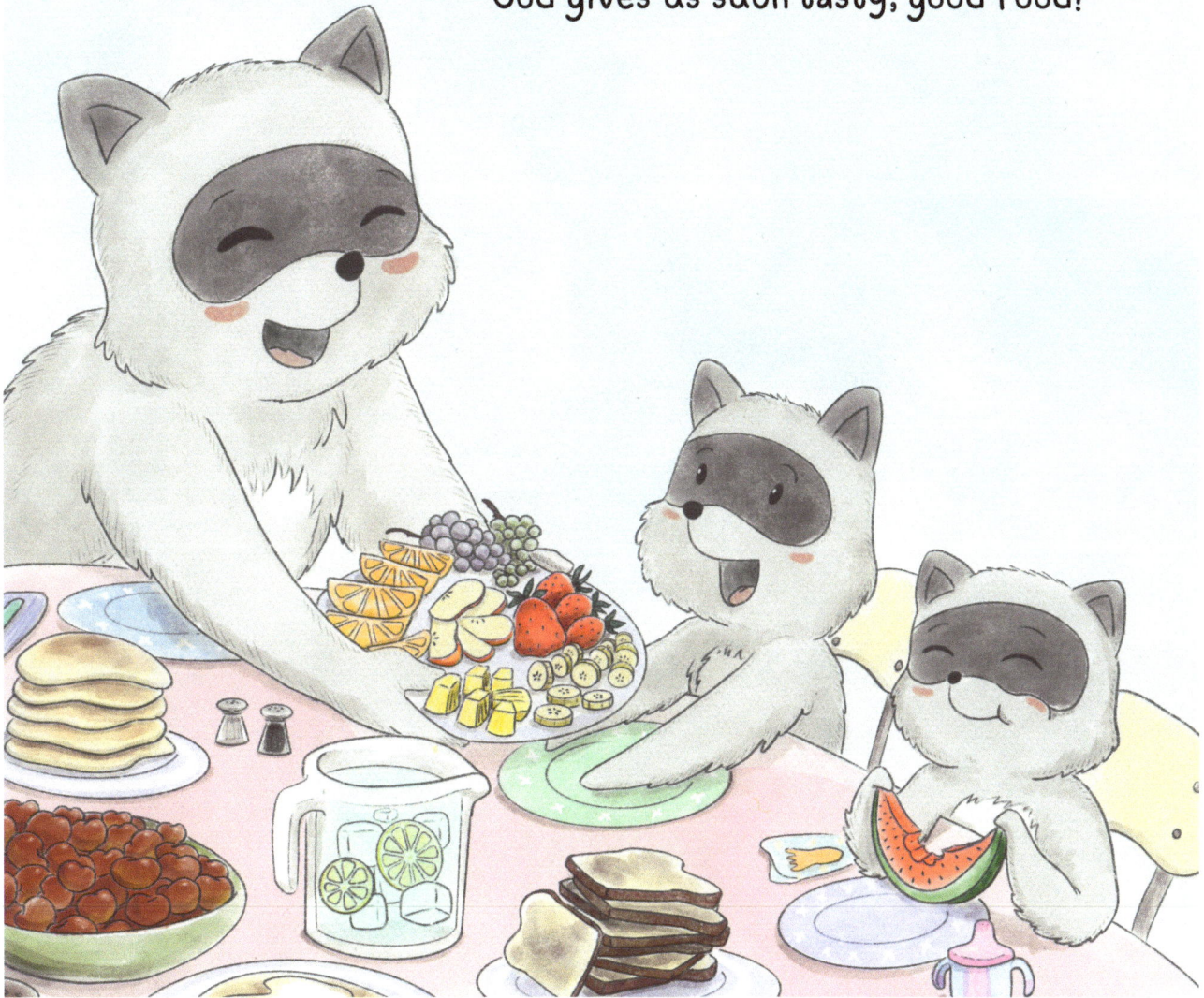

You might spruce up—not a wrinkle or spot.
But I like more crumply styles.

Whether we're fancy or whether we're not,
Let's dress up our faces with smiles.

I follow snails, with their slimy-slime trails,
While others chase butterflies flitting.

You may like puppies
that pounce their own tails.

Or do you find
kittens more fitting?

Maybe you're messy
and not a good sorter.
(With stuff scattered
over your floor!)

Some might be neater
and like things in order.
(They know what a hamper is for!)

People are different
 as autumn from spring;
Some brawny, some frail,
 and some weak.
Some just like humming
 while others will sing ...
God made every person unique.

Naptime means quiet,
    but you still can choose,
When you're all alone
    in your bed ...
Maybe you daydream
    and don't like to snooze—
You plan out
    adventures instead.

Tea-party mornings, and truck afternoons ...

We all get to play what we like.

I might make music with bowls and some spoons,
While you take a ride on your bike.

Writing or drawing with pencils or chalk—
We choose what we want to create.
Paint a bright picture or polish a rock—
It's yours, so it's sure to be great!

Some art is messy, and some is refined,
And some pieces might earn acclaim.
Art is like you—it is one of a kind—
Creations are never the same.

Owl

Reading good stories
   on wet, drizzly days ...
Or dinosaur dancing in puddles.
Some prefer playing in standoffish ways,
But others may want hugs and cuddles.

Some folks like dinner all mashed like potatoes—
they smush everything
that they eat.

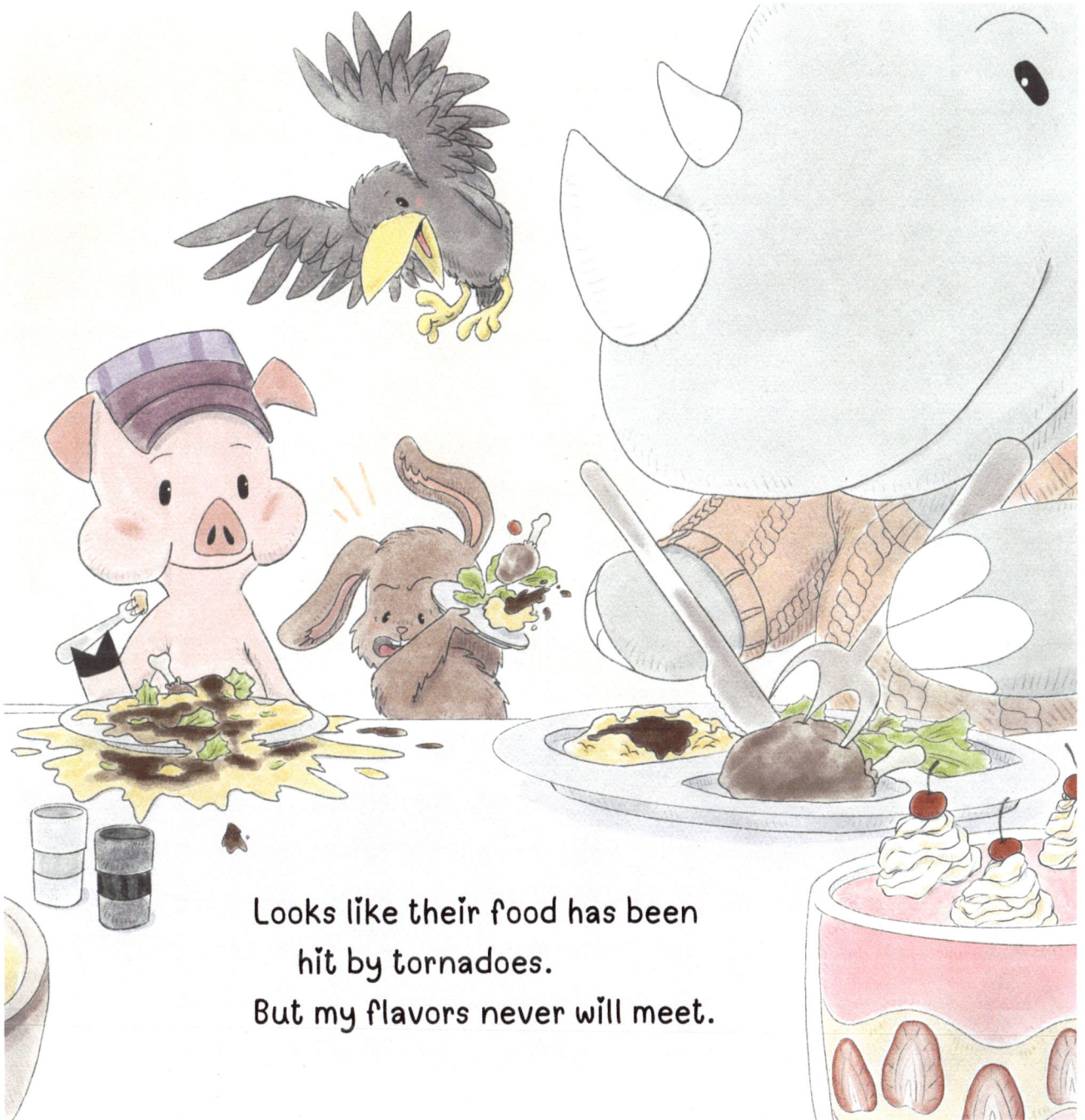

Looks like their food has been
hit by tornadoes.
But my flavors never will meet.

You enjoy doing some things that I don't.
That's fine—it's not sinful or strange.

I will try plenty of things that you won't.
That's nothing that we need to change.

People are different, as leather from lace—
  some rowdy, some mousy, some meek.
God made this world,
  such a beautiful place—
He made every person
  unique!

This book was published by Paraklesis Press--a small press committed to creating delightful children's books that are printed in America, with messages that lean, if they lean at all, to the right of center.

To order copies direct from the publisher go to ParaklesisPressBooks.com. Discounts available for bulk orders; write to sales@ParaklesisPress.com for details.

Independent publishers rely on online reviews to help sell their books. So, if you liked this book, you can help the author a ton, by leaving a review on Amazon, Goodreads, or wherever you buy and discuss books.

If you'd like to be entered to win books and merch from Paraklesis Press, please sign up for a our monthly newsletter at ParaklesisPress.com/updates or use the handy, dandy QR code. We pick one winner each month from all our newsletter subscribers.

Thanks ever so much!

www.ingramcontent.com/pod-product-compliance
Lightning Source LLC
Chambersburg PA
CBHW060845270326
41933CB00003B/201